Wipe-Clean

I can COUNT

Parragon

Bath · New York · Cologne · Melbourne · Delhi
Hong Kong · Shenzhen · Singapore · Amsterdam

This edition published by Parragon Books Ltd in 2015

Parragon Books Ltd
Chartist House
15–17 Trim Street
Bath BA1 1HA, UK
www.parragon.com
Please retain this information for future reference.

Copyright © Parragon Books Ltd 2015

Written by Emily Stead   Illustrated by Dan Taylor

ISBN 978-1-4748-0216-1

Printed in China

Contents

Big and small

Put a tick by the things that are small.

Which one is smaller and which one is bigger?

Put a cross by the things that are big.

Long, short and tall

Put a tick by the shortest caterpillar.
Put a cross by the longest caterpillar.

Look at the snowmen. Put a tick by the shortest snowman. Put a cross by the tallest snowman.

Draw lines to join each snowman to its matching scarf.

One, two, three

Draw dots in the bottom halves to match the numbers.

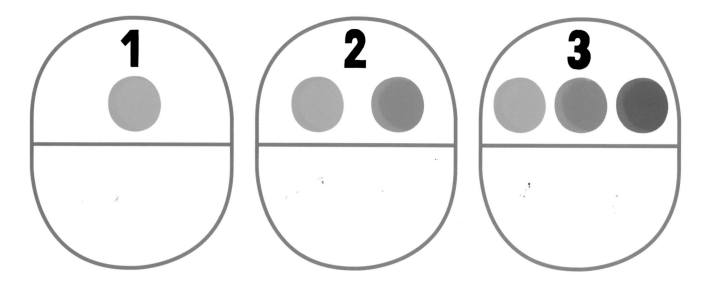

Write in the missing number.

Say the numbers out loud!

How many?

Draw circles around the correct numbers.

How many elephants?

1
2
3

How many teddy bears?

1
2
3

Three pigs

Draw lines to join each pig to the correct-sized house.

Draw lines to join each pig to the correct-sized mug.

Count four

Point to each balloon as you count them.
Trace the number.

Count how many apples.
Draw a circle around the correct number.

1 2 3 4

Draw a circle around the number
of windows on the boat.

1 2 3 4

Count the aeroplane windows. Draw a circle around the aeroplane with four round windows.

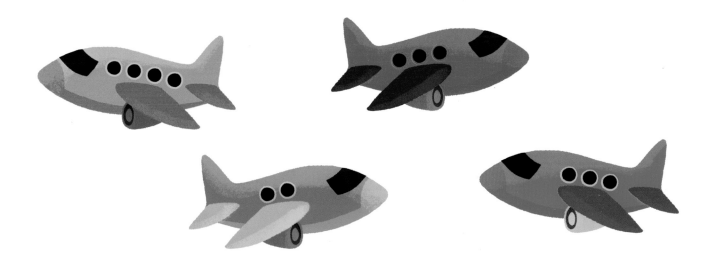

Look at the picture. Tick the box for runner number four.

Count five

Point to each lollipop as you count them.
Trace the number.

Look at the hand. Count how many fingers.
Draw a circle around the correct number.

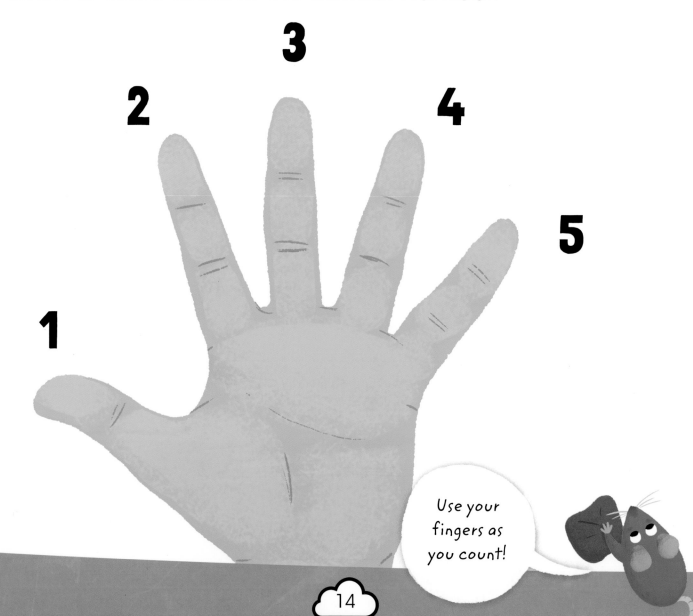

Use your fingers as you count!

Draw a circle around the dog with five spots.

Draw five biscuits on the plate.

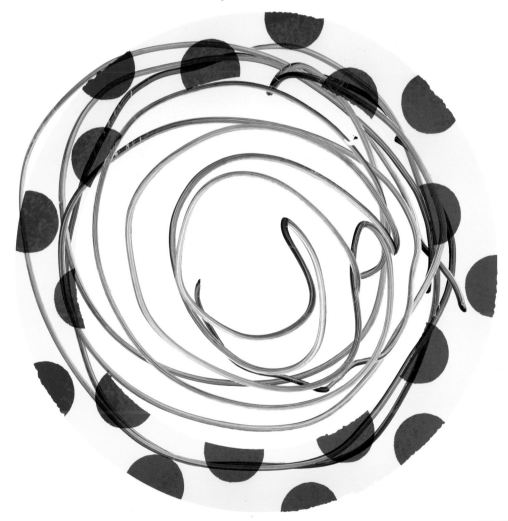

Three, four, five

Draw dots in the bottom halves to match the numbers.

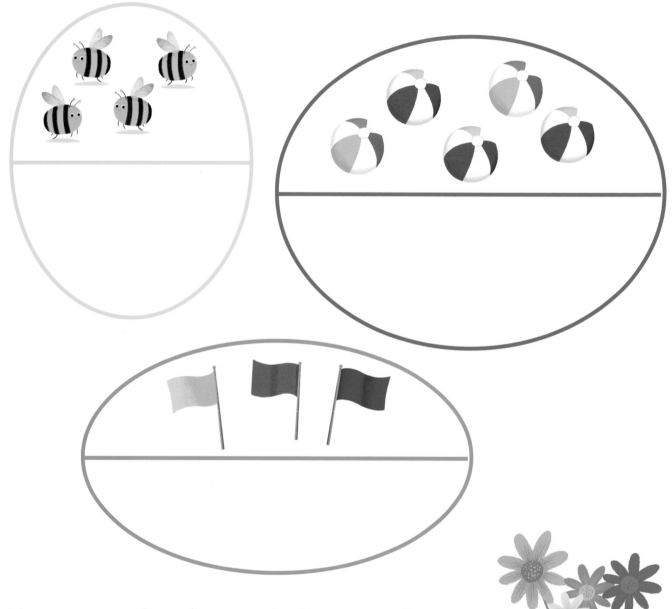

How many flowers are in the vase?
Draw a circle around the correct number.

3   4   5

Count the cups in each set.
Draw lines to join each set to the right number.

1

2

3

4

5

Practise counting with real cups!

Circles

Trace the dotted lines with your pen.
Which circle is the smallest? Put a tick inside it.
Which circle is the biggest? Put a cross inside it.

They are different sizes and colours, but they are ALL circles!

Look at the picture and find the circles.
Draw around them.

Squares

Trace the dotted lines with your pen.
Count the sides of the squares – 1, 2, 3, 4.

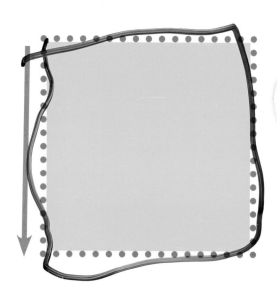

Squares have four equal sides!

Put a tick inside the smallest square.
Put a cross inside the biggest square.

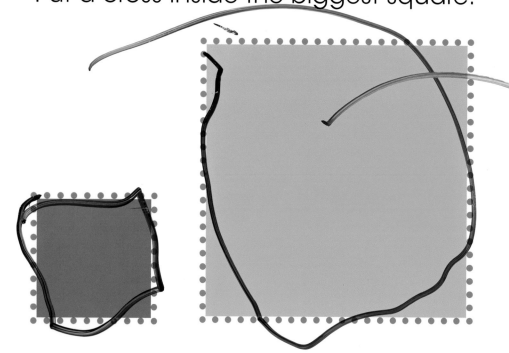

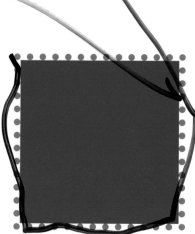

Find the squares in this picture.
Draw around them.

Triangles

Trace the dotted lines with your pen.
Now count the sides of the triangles – 1, 2, 3.

All triangles have three sides.

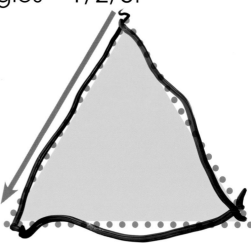

Draw over the dotted lines to finish each triangle.

Draw over the dotted lines to reveal some more triangle shapes.

Shapes and colours

Look at the pictures. Draw around each shape.
Say the name of each shape.

 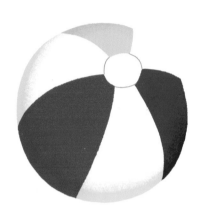 

These shapes make two patterns.
Draw two more shapes to finish the patterns.

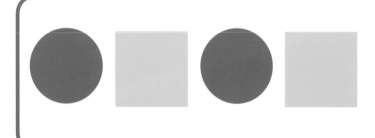

Match the shapes

Draw lines to join each object to its shape.

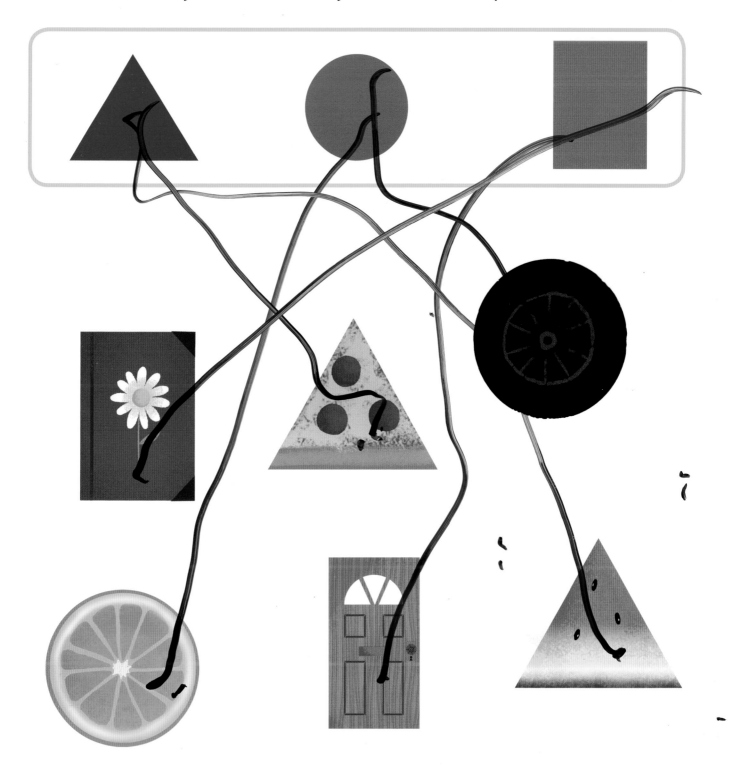

Up and down

Count up the levels of the beehive.
Count back down again.

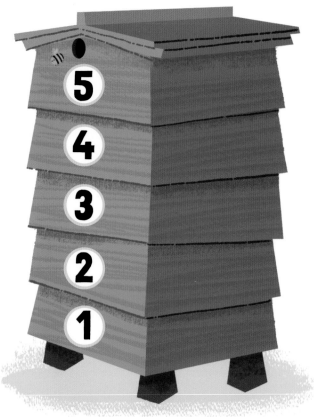

Count the black stripes on each bee.
Draw lines to join each bee to the
same number on the beehive.

Fill in the missing numbers on the snake.
Draw lines to join the dots to the right numbers.

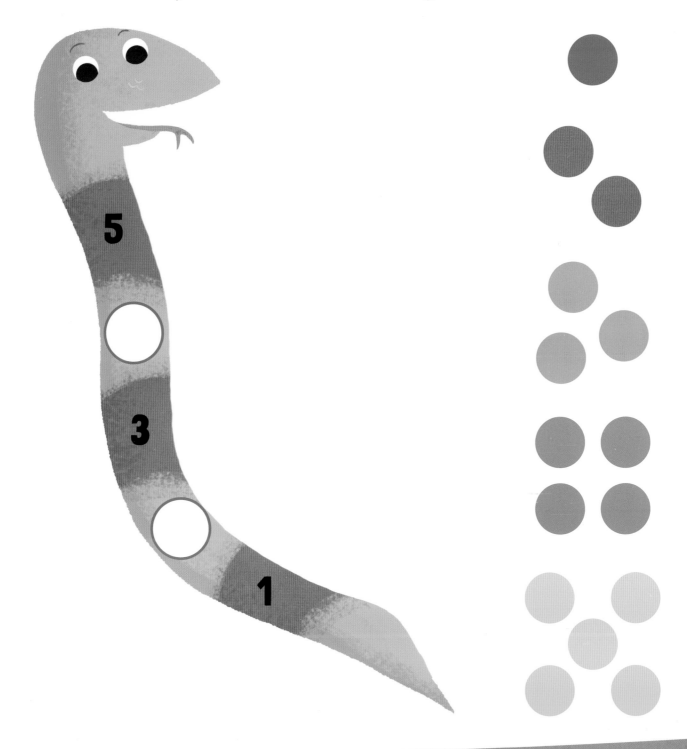

The same

Count the spots on each ladybird. Draw lines to join the ladybirds with the same number of spots.

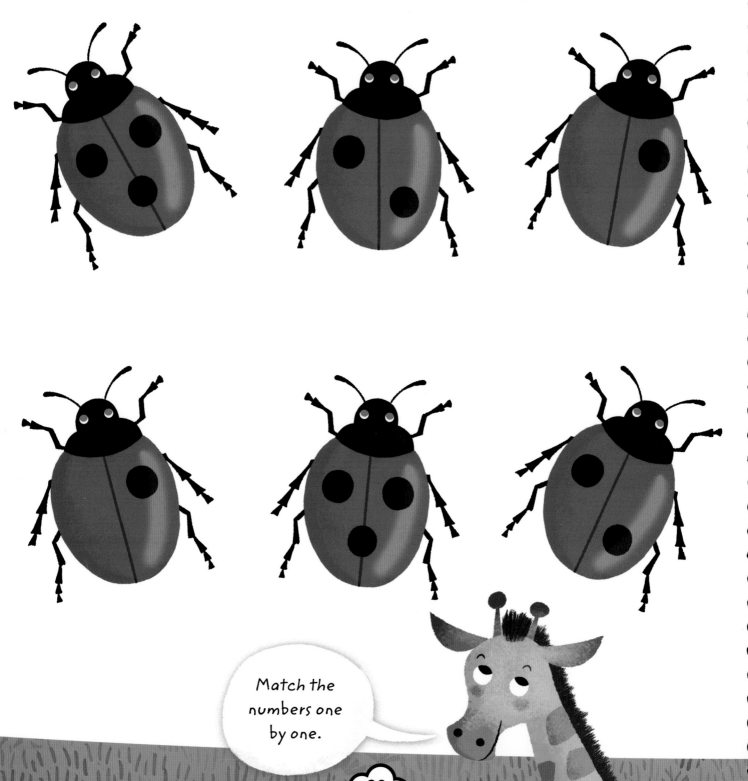

Match the numbers one by one.

Another one

Each monkey needs a banana. Draw one more.

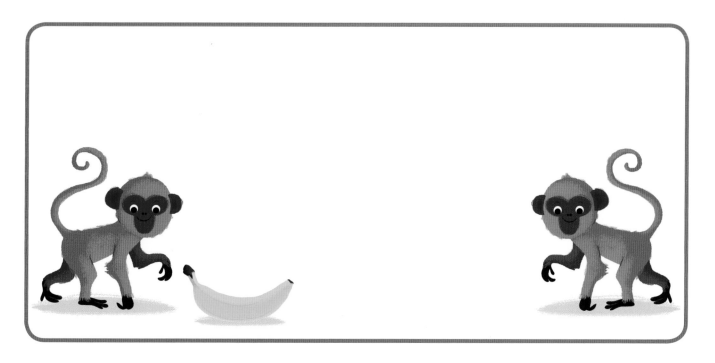

Each web needs a spider. Draw one more.

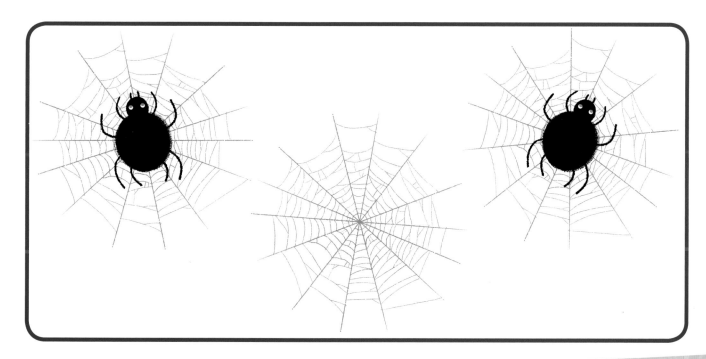

One add one

Point to each picture and count the objects.
Say the numbers out loud.

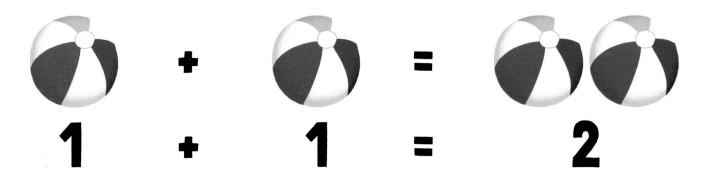

1 + **1** = **2**

One and one make two.

2 + **1** = **3**

Two and one make three.

Write numbers in the boxes to make the totals.

 +  =

1 + **1** =

 +  =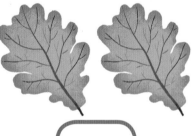

1 + **1** =

Follow the sums
with your fingers
as you say them.

One more

Draw one more sock.

 How many socks are there altogether?

Draw one more book.

  How many books are there altogether?

Draw one more mug.

How many mugs are there altogether?

Draw one more biscuit.

How many biscuits are there altogether?

Add one

Point to each picture and count the objects.
Say the numbers out loud.

One and one make two.

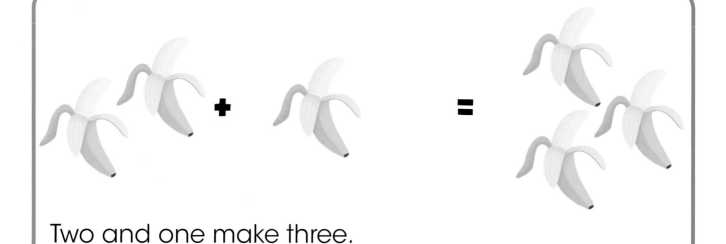

Two and one make three.

The last picture
shows the total.

Three and one make four.

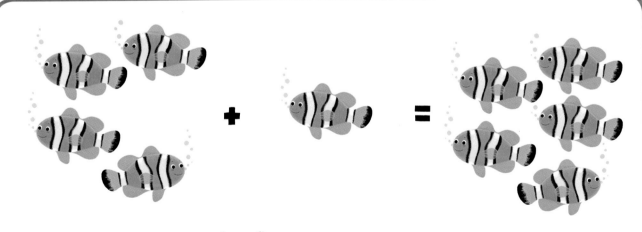

Four and one make five.

More or less

Look at the pictures. Draw a line to join the two trains with the same number of carriages.

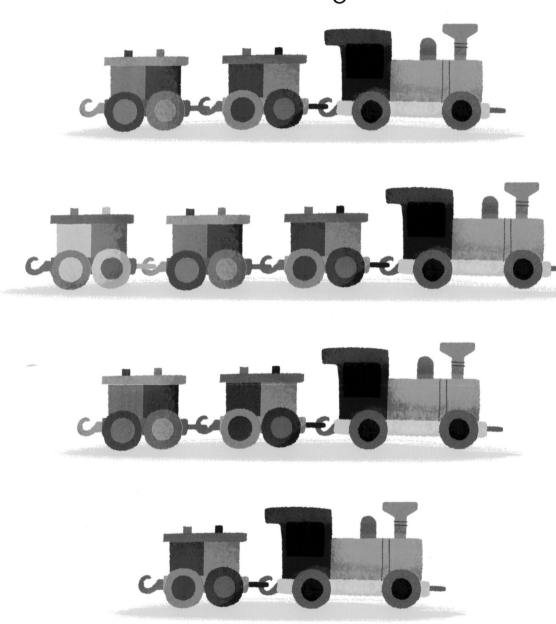

Draw around the train with the most carriages.

Count the scoops of ice cream in each cone. Yum!
Tick the cone with one less scoop.

Count the lollipops in the jar.
Tick the jar with one more lollipop.

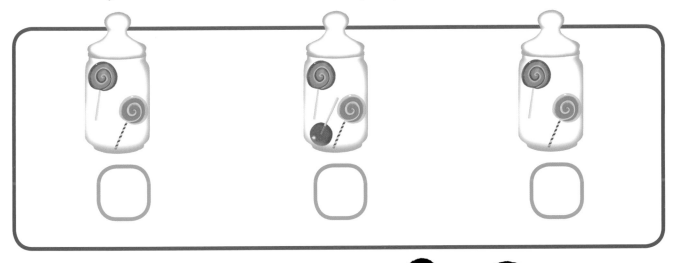

Which one has less and which one has more?

Take one away

Point to each picture and count. Then take away one and write the numbers in the boxes.

☐ take away one leaves ☐

☐ take away one leaves ☐

☐ take away one leaves ☐

take away one leaves

take away one leaves

You can use real pieces of fruit to practise taking away!

take away one leaves

Answers

Pages 4-5

Pages 6-7

Page 8
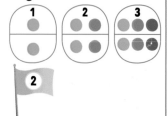

Page 9
2 elephants and 3 bears

Pages 10-11

Pages 12-13
4 apples and 4 windows

Pages 14-15
5 fingers

Pages 16-17
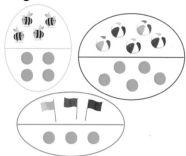

5 flowers
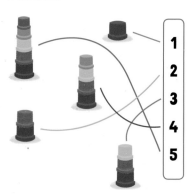

Page 18
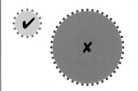

Page 20
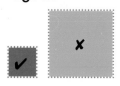

Page 24

Page 25

Pages 26-27
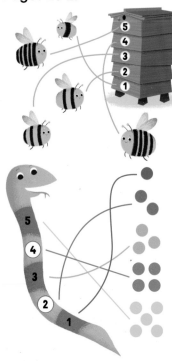

Page 28
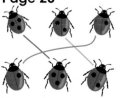

Page 31
1 sock + 1 sock = 2 socks
1 leaf + 1 leaf = 2 leaves

Pages 32-33
2 socks, 3 books, 4 mugs and 5 biscuits

Page 36
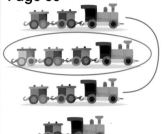

Page 37

Pages 38-39

5 take away one leaves 4

3 take away one leaves 2

4 take away one leaves 3

4 take away one leaves 3

2 take away one leaves 1

3 take away one leaves 2